Fun Educational Games for Kids

Innovative Ways for Parents to Teach Kids Using Educational Games

By: Sandy Harper

9781630225759

I0423626

TABLE OF CONTENTS

Sandy Harper

PUBLISHERS NOTES

All rights reserved. In accordance with the U.S. Copyright Act of 1976, the scanning, uploading and electronic sharing of any part of this book without the explicit written consent or permission of the publisher constitutes unlawful piracy and the theft of intellectual property.

If you would like to use material or content from this book (other than for review purposes), prior written permission must be obtained from the publisher.

You can contact the publishing company at admin@speedypublishing.com. Thank you for not infringing on the author's rights.

Speedy Publishing LLC

40 E. Main St., #1156

Newark, DE 19711

www.speedypublishing.co

Cover Artwork: 24 Hr. Designs Ltd.

Editing: Speedy Publishing LLC

Book design: Speedy Publishing LLC

ISBN: 9781630225759

This is a reprint book.

DISCLAIMER

This publication is intended to provide helpful and informative material. It is not intended to diagnose, treat, cure, or prevent any health problem or condition, nor is intended to replace the advice of a physician. No action should be taken solely on the contents of this book. Always consult your physician or qualified health-care professional on any matters regarding your health and before adopting any suggestions in this book or drawing inferences from it.

The author and publisher specifically disclaim all responsibility for any liability, loss or risk, personal or otherwise, which is incurred as a consequence, directly or indirectly, from the use or application of any contents of this book.

Any and all product names referenced within this book are the trademarks of their respective owners. None of these owners have sponsored, authorized, endorsed, or approved this book.

Always read all information provided by the manufacturers' product labels before using their products. The author and publisher are not responsible for claims made by manufacturers.

Sandy Harper

DEDICATION

Hey Cathy! I had you in mind. Try these things out - both you and the kids.

CHAPTER 1- EDUCATIONAL TOYS FOR YOUR CHILD

Educational toys are a great way to stimulate a child's mind.

When it comes to your children, you want the best for them.

In a sense, you want them to start to learn as soon as possible, learning the good things in life as well as the bad things. So why not teach them how to play with baby dolls that can guide them to learning human behaviors, including languages.

Dolls that can talk in different languages and teach them many things can help them to interact well with cultures, race and others that surround them each day.

What are some of the dolls that can teach your children?

These dolls that can teach your children many things are called teach-a-tot boy and girl. The dolls are for the ages of eighteen months to thirty-six months. Each doll has something to offer your child. Pattie, Lizzie and others have seven points that your child can press that will catch their eyes. The toys produce huge stars of shades of yellow that appear on the shoes.

Pattie talks, she says things like I can blow my nose. This teaches your child that it is ok to blow his or her nose. It is natural. What a great idea, since many children today fear the notion of expressing humane qualities. Lizzie and Pattie will tell your child when she has to go potty also. This helps your child to notice when bodily functions are at work, and helps them by encouraging potty training.

"I can brush my hair," says Liz and Pat. The dolls will also tell your child that she can brush her teeth. What a great way to help your child learn personal hygiene.

Liz and Pat are small figurines that have friendly smiles that light up your child's face. The soft, weighted material is easy for your child to lift and carry, as she likes.

Pat and Liz have removable garments; which teaches your child the importance and methods in dressing. Liz and Pat also have huge buttons that attach her shirt, which teaches your child how to unbutton and button attire. Pat's and Liz have shoes that your child can tie or untie, teaching them basic human skills. Your child will learn to zip, tie, dress, brush hair and more while playing with Liz and Pat. The dolls come complete with tissue, clothing, toothbrush, comb and more.

Boys look out Pat and Liz has a counterpart:

They have some dolls that will help to teach your children different languages as well as teach them things like tying shoes, unbutton, and button clothes. The child learns basic skills as well as new languages. The dolls speak French, Hebrew, Japanese, Russian as well as English. These dolls are called Lizzie dolls and they talk in many languages as they teach your child basic skills.

Aside from dolls you will find other toys online that teach your child basic human skills, which they develop as they practice with the toys. Some of the latest inventions include board games, videos, DVD, CD, building toys and more. Whatever your child desires or mostly what your child needs to develop you will find a wide array of toys online.

Children have advantages these days, since now they can get ahead of technology. While technology is constantly building new learning tools, children who start learning now gets ahead since they prepare for the next arrival.

Technology has also designed toys for all ages, including baby toys, toddlers and preschoolers. It is nice knowing that your child can learn healthy skills with toys instead of knowing they learn about violence and other unhealthy skills in the world.

CHAPTER 2- EDUCATIONAL TOYS IN COMPUTER TECHNOLOGY

As technology improves, more and more things are being created to help children learn. Technological toys have been especially for children with special needs.

Computers are everywhere these days and our children can learn many new things at any age. Our children need to stay up with the times and even one step ahead in order to stay connected with the world of computer and learning.

It is never too early to teach our children new things. Making learning fun is what it is all about. Computer and software can teach just about anything you want it to be. Searching has to be done to find the right one for that right person and on the Internet is a good place to start. There are so many different programs out today that choosing the right one will take some time and effort.

Reading is hard for a lot of us even as adults let alone your child that are just starting. Turn they're reading skills over by getting a program called Fonty for all age groups. Fonty will teach them new skill you didn't think was possible.

This program will teach them by using colorful animations, graphics, syllables and sentences by making games and exercises even and test for them to take on what they have learned. This software will teach your child to work with up to 600 words and sentences. The computer will talk to your children and they can talk back. Fonty has been known to teach children and adults that have a learning disability to read and have fun.

Your child or even yourself may be taking Physics and struggling to get through. Check this one out it is called Physics 1 Plus program. Teaching them and letting them learn at their own pace. Physics 1 will teach them energy, force, dynamics, wave's gravity and many other things. The lessons are clear and simple using animations, videos making the lessons easier giving quizzes along the way.

Scholastic Brain Play is for grades 1 through 3. Brain Play will teach your child math, science, reading and computer skills too. Famous characters are used to keep the learning fun along with 4 CD's and workbooks.

Leap Frog History and Geography learning for the 4th grade level. Using the Leap Frog pad and pencil along with the cartridge to go with the book teaches your child history and geography of the United States. Start your child out early like in the 3rd grade teaching them that learning can be fun they will be ahead when they start the 4th grade.

Sandy Harper

Early Learning Adventure is for the kindergartner that is just starting school. This program will teach your child the skill he or she will need to start leaning in a new environment along with simple math, science, and reading skills.

Peter Rabbit for grades 4 through 6th will help your child the skill for math. It teaches them the value of numbers in a fun way.

Disney is games about finding food for the animals; sing along with the music, writing a story with Tarzan.

Letting your child learn by having fun is what it's is all about. Learning new skills with each program, you invest in to put on your computer. Learning more computer skills is as important and reading to keep up with the times.

The True Blue Friend program put out by the Super Kids is about whales. With 2 games, one is matching parts of different flukes and a puzzle putting 40 different pictures together taken from the learning lessons. The story is about an old blue whale that turns his back on a young humpback whale. The CD-ROM that is included will teach skills of math, science, and reading to your child. This program is for the K through 2nd grades.

Search and find the program for your children to make learning and computers fun.

CHAPTER 3- EDUCATIONAL TOYS HOW THEY HELP WITH CAREER CHOICES IN THE FUTURE

Educational toys will not only help to open up a child's mind and foster learning but can also help them o determine what they would like to do when they grow up (teacher, doctor, lawyer or business entrepreneur).

Kids everyday wonder the earth say, "When I grow up," I am going to be a doctor. Some children feel a need to test science while others have an inner gift that drives them to learn, learn, and learn some more. Sometimes we have to help the little tots, since the world offers them too many choices it is sometimes difficult to decide what one wants to be when they grow up. Instead of letting your child become dragged down with burden of decision, find a way to help your child learn how to make sound decisions that makes him or her feel like a complete person. This is part of development, which takes place each day. In a world filled with chaos, your child needs a lighter load to carry on his or her shoulder. Take off the weight and head to the toy store where you will find educational toys to galore.

Thanks to the Internet, we have a wide range of toys to help our children decide their future as well as learn new skills that helps them along in life. Many toys today are affordable, making it easy for parents to buy their children a variety, which gives them the option of choosing their own. Today our children have choices of VHS, DVD, and CDs, books, illustration books, laptops, electronic learning toys and more. No matter what your child likes technology has designed something for your child.

Sandy Harper
How educational toys help your child's development:

It depends on the toy, yet your child can develop new skills from most educational toys designed today. Educational toys today can give your child the ability to see life in a complete new way. Your child will learn focus and awareness with some toys that helps them to spot new events that take place in their presence. Your child can develop points of views in a complete new light, as well as find maturity more fun. Maturity is frightening, especially when we live in an undeveloped world that fails to teach the children the entirety of what maturity brings. Children see death, illness, and accidents and so on each day on television, in the news, or even around them. Our children often lack developmental skills; which denies them the chance to live a productive, healthy lifestyle when they become adults. It takes us as parents to help our children develop the skills they need to "walk-the-walk" of life with success following them along.

Unfortunately, more children today suffer since they lack development, or mental illnesses take over their life. On this note, technology came up with solutions that make child development something that children will enjoy. Some of the most fascinating toys available today include the Cognitive Play. The toys help your child develop cognitive thinking skills, which promotes awareness. Your child will learn to think for self as he or she learns a system of organization that helps the child control his or her mind.

Cognitive toys help your child develop language, which promotes communication. Your child will learn how to use his or her imagination to reason, solve problems, come up with new ideas and think for self. This means that your child's memory will improve. Our children grow up in a world, which they go through a learning process each day they wake up. The learning process is gained from parents, natural inborn gifts, such as instincts, influences around them, television, and radio and so on. To help your children learn developmental skills that teach them how to survive, parents has to find the right tools that guide both the child and parent to a successful path down life's long-winding highway. Help your child decide what he or she wants to be when they grow up.

CHAPTER 4- EDUCATIONAL TOYS PLUS

Educational Toys help to develop the fine motor skills of a child.

Back in the day, we had the Baby Alive Dolls, which fed and drank. The dolls taught little girls how to take care of a baby. The doll would eat baby food and dispose of it by releasing feces. Now, we have a wide array of educational toys that promote child development beyond learning how to take care of an infant. Today we have toys that teach our children how to manipulate a vehicle. We have toys that train our children how to use their thinking skills. In addition, we have toys that help our children develop learning skills, which include math, reading, writing, history and more.

Online you will find a wide array of educational toys that benefit your child in many ways, helping you also through the process of child development. Toys are available for all ages. If you are searching for educational toys for your three-year-old child, you may want to consider the colorful toy boxes. The boxes contain over twenty sequential puzzles made into a card and teaches your child the cycle of life.

How your child benefits?

Your child benefits from this toy, since he or she learns how to move objects to the left and to the right. Right and left-hand learning is the point to this educational toy. Yet, there is more. The puzzle parts differ, making the cards a self-correct model for learning precision. The goal is to teach your child through a fun, learning process the causes and effects of life. What a great way to teach your child consequences for his or her decisions and behavior.

The cards also show your child how to develop reason skills. Your child will have fun while he or she learns how to make good choices. In addition, the cards teach your child culture. The bi-lingual cards come in both Spanish and English teaching. Your child also learns how to think logically. The cards help the child by allowing him or her to use association while considering problems. The skill your child obtains is cause and effect, association, logic and new languages.

Aside from the learning cards, you could teach your child how to become a mastermind in mathematics. The child will benefit from the latest Pirating treasure chests toys. Your child teaches division, addition, thinking skills, multiplications and subtractions while having fun. The Pirate games are ideal for children six and up. Your child will be the clever student as he or she enters 1st grade. Using gold coins, the game provides your child the ability to have fun while challenging simple to complex math questions. The game shows your child the results with the disk included.

In America, we have many children under developed. The educational toys today are designed to help parents teach their children developmental skills that benefit them throughout their life. Part of the world's problem is that children have babysitters called PlayStation, Nintendo, and television. Our children need more to grow healthy and strong. Instead of promoting to our children violent, immoral games and movies why not help your child grow into the next influential person in the future.

When your child develops learning skills, thinking skills and so forth, your child grows to a brilliant future. Your child as he or she matures will learn how to think for self and will make healthy decisions that take him or her down the road to success.

If you are in the progress, of helping your child develop healthy skills go online now and find your helper. Sometimes parents need help to train their children, which is why we have a wide array of educational toys today.

CHAPTER 5- THE BENEFITS OF TECHNOLOGY BASED EDUCATIONAL TOYS

Children love new things and they find things that they can interact with to be extremely interesting. The great thing is that they will be learning without even realizing it.

Technology has designed some amazing educational toys. On the Internet, you will find a wide array of toys that help your child develop new skills. The toys benefit parents and child, since it teaches them interaction skills, socialization, reading, writing, art, electronics, motor skills, hand and eye coordination, and more. Sit back and let technology take your child away from unruly activities that lead to nowhere but trouble. Today's games have promoted unruly behaviors that are leading children down a destructive path. Television and media promote unhealthy actions in many instances, thus technology had to work hard to guide our children back down the road to developing healthy, nature and useful skills.

Videos are available to help your child learn. Videos today include children's favorite Dora the lovely Explorer who takes your child along the maps through many adventures. Dora is available in audio/video. Dora takes your child on a journey with its digital structure through episodes of fun, including an adventure with the 3 favorite pigs, lost and the found, and through Nickelodeon's parental guides.

Your child will love episodes of the map that losses the huge bird from his goofy blunders. The bird has to gather his stick and fly around the map to find his nesting place that the Mountain's tallest point. Dora works along with Boots to find their way around the map, yet your friends need your help to draw a map that helps to rescue the bird. Using a Super, Duper Map Dora and her friend, Boots scurry along the trails heading back down from the mountaintop unwittingly knowing that a surprise awaits them at home. The funny Map character uses his magical cape and becomes Dora, Boots and your super-duper hero. Using his cape he flies above the majestic sky helping the friends find their way as he moves obstacles along the way with his super strengths and breathing tactics. What a great way to help your child learn how to find his or her way in life.

Get the blues from the clues as your child journeys onto school carrying on through loads of fun episodes to discover numbers? Your baby will enjoy the blues while he or she learns their math and alphabets. Travel along with Periwinkle and friends to learn how to discover new clues that helps your child solve problems, words and more. Your child will have hours of loaded fun as he or she travels down the road to school with Periwinkle and friends. Watch as Periwinkle works through his nervousness, using his friends Joe and Blue to pick him up. Reliance of others is something we all need sometimes which Periwinkle and friends teaches your child that it is ok to ask others for help. Your child will learn areas of school that interest him, as well as learn new strategies to help your child get through the hard times while learning. Using numbers the video will help your child learn favorites, as well as how to discover new favorites.

Pirates and music somehow goes hand-in-hand. Let Dora take your child on the Pirates adventures through musical environments where your child will expect loads of fun. Preschoolers will enjoy Dora as she moves along with Diego and her friend Boots enjoying the stars. Let your child learn about animals and nature as they enjoy the little tot jaguar who sings them a song. Pirates look out, since the pigs are out to steal your treasure chests. Get your chance to work along with Dora and friends so they can bring honesty and justice back to its place. Teach your child with Dora how to develop skills that bring them rewards in life.

CHAPTER 6- EDUCATIONAL TOYS- GAMES FOR GRADES SEVEN THROUGH TWELVE

Toys are created for specific age groups so a toy for a ten year old would be different from a toy for a toddler. Toys are created based on the expected level of development of the "typical child."

With the higher grades in mind, it can still be fun to learn new skill in game form. Games can prepare them for college; help them learn new skill while still in high school and having fun with their friends.

There are a lot of board games out that can entertain your teen and friends for many hours while they learn. Checking out the Internet is a good way to find educational toys for the older children to keep them interested in learning.

Strategy games can be a challenge to the teen you might be buying a gift for or just by giving. Strategy games will teach your child to think about their next move and how might that help them with the next. This teaches your child to think before doing, letting them have fun doing it.

Trivia games comes in a wide range of opportunities and challenges for the whole family even the one that has sports in their mind. This game teaches important facts and lets them use what they already know. Trivia comes by subject a game for the courtroom drama, or one with Bible facts so look around and see what one is best for your friend or family.

Government! Yes, I said Government in games is great to learn what is happening with the government. Pretend being the

President of the United States making decisions on how you would handle the situation. And lets you see and learn about the challenges of life in Washington DC. What a great way to learn about the United States.

Money games are very plentiful in different ways. Each one will teach your child how to handle money, the value of money, counting, recognition, and giving change. Turn it into a family game night and teach your child the skills they need with handling money.

Word games are fun and children can learn to spell. The race up the hill with work challenges helps them to figure out a way to get over it and find the next one. Word games come in all grade levels from grade 1 and up. Some word games for grades 9 through 12 will include words and numbers. Making decisions with everyday problems to work out is often difficult for a child.

Maze puzzle games are challenges by testing the abilities, patience and challenges to get to the end. Challenging their friends is fun to see who can find their way out first.

For the sports, person in your life give sports trivia game. These trivia games come in any sport you can imagine. Let them challenge their friends to see who know more than the other about their favorite sport does. Teaches them think and the skill of getting along with others too learning new facts and having fun:

Educational Brainteasers will test your patience and skills along with teaching you to have fun and learn at the same time. These games are stimulating, entertaining as well as educational. You might be trying to match geometric figures with one hand and align magnets with the other. That would be a challenge and using coordination too.

Sandy Harper

Learn sign language in game form. You'll learn to talk and sing along with the CD's that come with it using your hands. Challenge your friends and see if they can tell what you're saying to them.

Trying out your patience with a logic game will teach your child how to manage his or her emotions. These boards come in all shapes and sizes making you analyze yourself and enrich your reasoning. Logic games come in all age groups including the graduate in a challenge of playing chess on a circular board.

CHAPTER 7- LAPTOPS IN EDUCATIONAL TOYS

A laptop used to be for adult only but as the benefits of its use are being realized, they are now being created to help kids learn.

Laptop toys come in all age ranges for 2 years and up. Start your child out early using a toy laptop to help get them prepared for the years to come. Computers and technology toys are becoming more advanced every day and your child needs to be ready. Laptops help your child's self-esteem and confidence making them proud and feel like a big kid.

Children need to grow with the flow and learning as early as 2 can give them a head start to the new toys ahead. Learning and teaching your child new things should be fun and give them a challenge as well. Laptops are a great way to prepare them to use the computer, learn to play games with a fun challenge, coordination will improve, learning skills like thinking to solve something, and keep them one step ahead of the world of technology.

Laptops come in many different styles, different way to teach your child, colors, making learning fun by sitting next to mom or dad when they are on their computer. This will inspire your child to bond with mom and dad while he or she learns new skills.

With the younger children in mind preparing them to start school the Electronic Alphabet Book is a nice laptop teaching for teaching your child the basics. This laptop will make learning the alphabet fun, along with learning their numbers, spelling out words, and animals with the sounds they make. The price is right on this laptop so if something happens to it or they outgrow it soon after getting you won't be out a lot of money and the child has learning from it.

For the middle age, groups that are learning math and other learning skills check out the Educational Laptop for Kids. This computer is the top of the line in children's computers for beginners. Getting a laptop that teaches your child the basic math, and English skills are great. This Laptop for kids is a great one because it also has 8 different games to let them use their new skills and coordination at the same time. Music skills are also included in the laptop teaching the Christmas songs and children songs 90 total songs in all. Learning to play and read music can be fun with the piano lessons; who knows your child might want to play in an orchestra some day or want to become a singer. Calculators are needed in most all grades today; and now is the time for them to learn how to use one. A calculator is included on it teaching them how to check their math with it.

In today world, everyone should know a second language. Spanish is a good one for your child to learn because there are a lot of Spanish speaking people that are learning to speak English. Give your children the chance to learn Spanish so they can communicate with their friends at school or anywhere else. The Education Spanish Learner is on the top of the list. This laptop is like the Laptop for Kids having all the same things only it will teach them to speak in Spanish. Your child will learn the skills of another language and it will be fun.

Educational Laptops with a mouse is nice. More coordination is being used with the mouse and they will still be learning all the basic skills they will need in school. This one also comes with English and Spanish on it. Look at all the learning skills here coordination, math, English, spelling, calculator, games, piano lessons and songs to teach singing skills along with teaching the Spanish language.

Chapter 8- Leapfrog the Educational Toys for Child Development

Leapfrog developmental toys are extremely popular and with good reason as they help children to learn to read and count and learn their colors with ease.

As a child do you remember seeing a toy that you love to play, one that would help you to learn your letters help you to write your name, count and so forth? Today there is a wonderful toy that is out that will also help your child to do that same thing they just have more technology in them making them better for your child to learn faster.

How does the Leapfrog help my child learn?

Leapfrog has many toys that will help your child to learn the basic things they need to know to go to school. This wonderful toy is called leapfrog fridge phonic magnetic letter with numbers.

This toy is for the ages of two and up. Therefore, kids of all age's even moms and dad can enjoy the frog as he leaps. The Leapfrog's include the ABC and 1, 2, 3. The frogs go where magnetic go.

They will stick and let your child move them in any way they want. The Leapfrog will spell words, such as cat, dog and more plus there are the numbers spoken, which helps your child to learn to count.

When the child spells a word the magnetic tells them what word they spelled. This will help them to spell as well as read. The numbers will help your child to learn to count they will repeat the order they are in and then say the order that they are supposed to be in.

The letter and numbers are very colorful as well. This frog talks and sings songs. Just think of all the fun your child will have playing with this toy, make it easier for you to do what you have to do around the house.

Another toy that is almost the same as this but it is a school bus. The School bus helps your child to develop new skills they need to start the first day of school.

It is for the age's three to five. This school bus will help them to pre read as well as pre write. Therefore, this is also a good toy to get your child along with the magnetic frog.

The toy is available in several platforms. Instead of purchasing one shaped like a school bus, you can buy character shaped items, such as Dora the Explorer. The wiggles and the famous Sponge bob square pants are available also. Therefore, if one of these characters is your child's favorite, it will make your child inspired as he or she will have fun while learning.

How will these toys help my child to learn?

Like with everyone else if your child is interested in something they are going to play with it repeatedly. By doing this it will finally teach them things and once they start to learn, they will continue to do so. Most children learn from being told something repeatedly, which is the prime purpose these toys were designed.

Where do I go to get these educational toys?

These educational toys are in all the stores like your local Wal-Mart, Kmart, Rite-Aid, and Walgreen's and so on. You can order

Sandy Harper

from these stores online. As well, you will find Toy-r-Us and other kid stores online that probably carry the Leapfrog, school bus and related toys.

Various stores online may offer you coupons, which allows you to save money while helping your child develop new skills. Sometimes you can find closeouts online, which enables you to buy name brand toys half the price. In addition, promotional campaigns are always going online, which gives you advantages of saving money.

CHAPTER 9- LEAPING WITH EDUCATIONAL TOY FROGS

The great thing about Leapfrog is that they have toys that can be used by a baby and also have toys for the older kids. They have covered all bases in child development.

Leapfrog is a great educational toy that helps your child to develop new skills.

Leaping with educational toy frogs can help your child learn:

Leapfrog is a very good toy to start your child out on, since it will help them to learn all kinds of things in early years. A baby starts to learn as soon as it is born so why not start them out at a youthful age. Leapfrog has many educational toys out there to help to teach your child all the skills he or she needs to know. Some educational toys that you can get to help your child as early as six months to thirty-six months will help them develop motor skills, sound, hearing, listening and other skills that benefit them.

What are some toys I can get to help my child learn?

The discover ball is one of the toys available that helps your child learn as early as six months plus. This ball is just a ball that the child can roll around the home. Yet, the ball teaches your child about chances. It does not balance so nothing should get broken unless someone throws it deliberately at something around the house.

Discovering the ball of letters and sounds:

The ball will help your child, by introducing him or her to letters, phonics, and motor skills. The ball helps your child to develop

Sandy Harper

motor skills, since he presses letters. The child learns the letters, since a press of one button provokes the toy to talk.

The ball allows your child to develop motor skills, since the child spins and rolls the ball, while hearing his or her alphabets. Your child can sing along. The ball teaches them three melodies.

Dazzling your child:

The lights flash to the beat of the music that the ball is playing; this will give them ability to build eye coordination.

More about the Leaping Learning Frogs:

Leapfrog is one of the learning toys, which is for the ages of six months to thirty-six months. This is a table, which the child can take the legs off and lay the learning parts on the floor. What a great way to spend time in the playpen.

Some of the things they might learn may be how to push, pull, slide, roll, and spin. It will also introduce them to about 40 different songs and melodies this will let your child sing to the songs while learning new sounds. Your child learns from sound, smell, sight and so on, what a great way to help your child develop new skills.

Leapfrogs also have a puppy that will teach your little ones how to cuddle while he or she is learning. This wonderful puppy will teach your little ones his or her A, B, C, as well as 1, 2, and 3. Your child will learn about body parts and ten different songs that will inspire them to enjoy the sounds of music while the child learns. The dog bone will light up also, lighting to the beat of the lyrics and music.

How do children learn from these toys?

Children learn from these toys when you start them at an early age since it helps them to develop their memory. When you combine early academic and everyday experience for the way kids learn it helps them to grow into who they become. Leapfrog has many other educational toys for all ages, to help children learn the basics skills they need to know. Starting your child out early in learning takes your child to a future filled with success.

CHAPTER 10- LEARNING WITH BOARD GAMES

Not to be scoffed at the board game is still a great way for a child to learn. It also brings family together.

Today your children learn with all types of toys and games. They learn some of the easiest things like how to count, read, their colors, and for the most, they learn how to play with others. They are learning at the same time having fun doing it.

How kids learn from playing broad games?

For the most part your child learns how to get along with other children. They learn that they cannot always win at something so this will help them to learn to share as well. They will learn the basics in reading, their colors, and how to count as well.

What are some of the games that my child might want to play?

There are many different kinds of board games that your child will enjoy playing.

Monopoly is a popular game to play as a family or as friends getting together. This game is for children ages 9 and up. As they play monopoly they learn all kinds of trades. One trade they might learn is how to use money to buy a house, motel or property to put it on. This game takes a long time to play, so a child with impatience may find it difficult to play the game. Although its one the Americans favorite board games today. Many people enjoy playing it as a family.

Another game your child may enjoy to play are the ones that represent their favorite characters, such as Dora the explorer.

Sponge Bob Square Pants, and Winnie the Pooh is some of the children's all-time favorite characters. Now your child can enjoy them on board games.

Another of the children's favorite games is Candy Land. Most kids of all ages will enjoy playing Candy Land as they learn new interacting skills.

Nowadays you can find board games that are similar to the ole' time favorite Candy Land. The new game is called Dora the Explorer. The game is played the same as you would play Candy Land. During the game, your child will learn how to count. The child will learn basic reading skills, as well as colors.

This game is for the ages of years old to 7 years old but you, as parents do not feel bad you can still play. In fact that would be a great thing to do is to play making it a family night. This will teach them how to spend quality time as a family.

Another board game, which is an oldie but goodie, is the Memory Games. This game is for child ages from 3 and up, which makes room for mom and dad to play also. Have fun as a family while you and your children spend quality time together.

This game will teach your child how to use their memory muscles. They will also learn how to use hand coordination. The children will learn by turning over the cards, trying to remember where they are and pairing them. The person that pairs the most wins the game. Take it easy on the little ones mom and dad.

Educational toys are a great way to learn. Other board games, includes Chess. Chess is a great board game that teaches your child how to use his or her thinking cap. Your child will learn manipulative skills while learning to use his or her critical mind to make his move.

Chess teaches children how to work as a team, yet separately as they try to checkmate his or her opponent. Chess is one of the most popular games played and in schools around the world; they are promoting this board game. To learn more about chess, go online and check out the educational toys waiting for you.

CHAPTER 11- LEARNING WITH ELECTRONIC EDUCATIONAL TOYS

Electronic toys have numerous advantages, from helping the child learn to speak to helping them learn how to do things like going to potty.

Today it is not hard to find an electronically toy that will help to teach your child all the great things to know before they start school. Some of the basic things your child can learn from electronic toys is counting, spelling, and learning their colors. Your child can learn shapes as well.

Today on the market, they have all these wonderful learning toys that help your child to learn new skills.

Most of the learning toys start as soon as your child can walk. Toys are available to help children age two and up learn new skills that guide them to a successful journey in elementary and up.

How does my child benefit from electronic toys?

Your child is going to love these toys. As they play, they will be learning and not even realizing that they are learning they will be having too much fun. The electronically toys today are made to teach your child some of the things that will make it easier for them in school. Your child will learn colors, shapes and how to count numbers with ease.

Some children do not have an interest in learning. Learning tends to make them feel bored. In the early years children relied on pen and paper, which made learning frustrating.

However, today they make learning fun for children. Technology has designed kids' computers that teach them new skills. The children will enjoy pictures, charts, graphics and more while they prance along through technology channels.

How do I choose electronic toys for my child?

One of the toys is called the chatterbox teaching phone this phone is a great way for your child to learn some communication skills. Your child can learn how to use the telephone, which gives them the benefit of interacting. Most children enjoy talking on the telephone. Telephones benefit your children since it teaches them communication skills, as well as interactive skills.

Telephones today teach your child to interact and communicate, as well as how to count numbers. Your child can learn shapes as well.

This toy comes in Spanish as well, which this will teach them to learn a new language. Chatterbox also comes in a thirty-puzzle card set. The puzzle will teach your child how to do math, learn colors and even shapes.

Your child may also enjoy the latest Bee Smart, which buzzes along making it fun for your child to learn spelling.

This is a toy to teach your child the wonders of spelling. The child will enjoy a selection of activities from phonics to spelling and learning letter quizzes. Your child can take his or her own spelling quiz and see their score. This is a great vocabulary builder for your child.

How will my kid develop from these toys?

Your child will learn new ideas and how to use his or her critical mind to make decisions. Your child will learn communication skills, since once he can spell and accomplish quizzes he or she will take off on to a new level of talking with others.

Electronic laptops are available for your children also. If your child enjoys surfing the Internet you will find electronic computers that allow him or her to connect the world of chattering. Your child can use the computer to research, play games, and learn new skills and more.

Where can I get these toys?

Buying the educational toys is easy today. You can find the toys nearly at any store that sells toys. They are very much in demand. Try using the Internet first however, since you will find clearances. Closeouts and other deals are available to you and your child also.

CHAPTER 12- LIFE SKILL IN EDUCATIONAL TOYS

Parents now have help to teach life skill and that is what the educational toy can do.

Educational toys come in many different categories teaching your children many things while letting them have fun learning.

Search the Internet to find a lot of different learning and skill toys. The Internet can provide you with a wide variety of ideas and toys to increase your child's knowledge in just about anything you want. If you're not sure on what kind of toy you're looking for just search for educational toys and you'll find articles everywhere to help you. Having fun is what buying for the children is all about. To enjoy your search and then once you have in mind what you're looking for go to a toy store and play with some of their displays giving you more fun and knowledge of what you are buying.

We all need to learn life skills in order to manage our lives. The earlier your child is taught some of these skills the better. Reading books is not always the ideal way to teach a child. Something new while having fun is great and rewarding way to teach everyone, Life skills can be taught through toys just like everything else these days.

Responsibility can be taught by giving a gift box as a gift to a child. The box has 2 keys in case one gets lost; it teaches the child responsibility by keeping track of the key for one thing. Everyone like their own privacy and a lock box is great for this to put their most cherished items into it and locking it up. What a great way to teach your child security.

Setting the table is something everyone needs to learn how to do; we all have to eat. A plastic set of dishes in many colors makes is fun to learn to set the table. After setting the table they can eat from them as well, this is something they can be proud of and stand back to see all the pretty colors. Using different colors they can learn to mix and match colors as well as learning the color itself.

Dates are important in all our lives even your children. Calendars made of cloth and the numbers and pictures all have a Velcro backing on them. Each month the child can move the dates' teaching them their numbers and teach them the seasons by sticking the sun on it for summer or a flower for spring. Special dates like birthdays can be stuck on, and learning the days of the week with a calendar is important to know what day it is. You can always cut out different thing from a magazine teaching your child to use scissors to add new things to their own personal calendar.

Their very own first aid kit is important to teach your child the skills of life. It is child friendly with a CD included to teach the first aid. Colorful Band-Aids and ointment are included too to make it fun.

Safety is something we all need to learn as early at 3 years old. Safety board is a race teaching the child how to get themselves out of different situations. They have to learn how to deal with strangers, what to do when lost, park rules, even learning when and how to dial 911.

A family game for the entire family, letting up to 4 people play at a time.

Teaching life skills are very important in today's world and making if fun is a whole lot better than letting them get into a situation that they don't know how to handle. The earlier these skills are taught the better to keep them safe and happy.

ABOUT THE AUTHOR

I believe there's so much we can learn during our average lifespan which is around 70 years old or so. From very young as a toddler, we can start learning and compound what we learn over the years. Anything that can aid us in doing that is something I'm usually interested in. The more we feed our brains the sharper our mind gets. There are so many techniques we can employ in order to bring this about so I'm really big on exploring those things and sharing what I find with others.

Even as I'm ageing, I'm more excited and not slowing down when it comes to things like brain exercises for memory improvement. Something as simple as doing puzzles or playing board games actually has an impact on keeping our minds sharp. It's really something that I encourage everyone to do. You are never too young or too old for brain stimulation in any way that you can get it.

www.ingramcontent.com/pod-product-compliance
Lightning Source LLC
Chambersburg PA
CBHW061805280526
45787CB00003BA/1487